THE LAPIDARY'S NOSEGAY

The Mountain West Poetry Series
Stephanie G'Schwind & Donald Revell, series editors

We Are Starved, by Joshua Kryah
The City She Was, by Carmen Giménez Smith
Upper Level Disturbances, by Kevin Goodan
The Two Standards, by Heather Winterer
Blue Heron, by Elizabeth Robinson
Hungry Moon, by Henrietta Goodman
The Logan Notebooks, by Rebecca Lindenberg
Songs, by Derek Henderson
The Verging Cities, by Natalie Scenters-Zapico
A Lamp Brighter than Foxfire, by Andrew S. Nicholson
House of Sugar, House of Stone, by Emily Pérez
&luckier, by Christopher J Johnson
Escape Velocity, by Bonnie Arning
We Remain Traditional, by Sylvia Chan
The Lapidary's Nosegay, by Lara Candland

LARA CANDLAND

THE LAPIDARY'S NOSEGAY

poems

The Center for Literary Publishing
Colorado State University

Printed in the United States of America.

Library of Congress Cataloging-in-Publication Data

Names: Candland, Lara, 1967- author.
Title: The lapidary's nosegay : poems / Lara Candland.
Other titles: Mountain west poetry series.
Description: Fort Collins, Colorado : The Center for Literary Publishing,
Colorado State University, [2018] | Series: The mountain west poetry series
Identifiers: LCCN 2017045630| ISBN 9781885635617 (pbk. : alk. paper) | ISBN
9781885635624 (electronic)
Subjects: | LCGFT: Experimental poetry.
Classification: LCC PS3603.A5373 A6 2018 | DDC 811/.6--dc23
LC record available at https://lccn.loc.gov/2017045630

The paper used in this book meets the minimum requirements of the American National Standard for Information Sciences-Permanence of Paper for Printed Library Materials, ANSI Z39.48-1984.

1 2 3 4 5   22 21 20 19 18

We play at Paste—
Till qualified for Pearl—
Then, drop the Paste—
And deem Ourself a fool—
The Shapes, tho', were similar,
And our new Hands
Learned Gem Tactics
Practising Sands—

—EMILY DICKINSON

TABLE OF CONTENTS

A KEY TO PARENTHETICAL AND OTHER MARKINGS

(	)	=	emphasis on *oh* or *oo* sound or non-essential clause.
((	))	=	listen, ears, wings, angels, birds, butterflies, ghosts with or without wings, any other winged creature or the Belle of Amherst is speaking.
(((	)))	=	petals, sun, pleasure, god, radiance, shine, gems.
((((	))))	=	unsaid, unanswered, ineffable, prayer, the Holy Spirit, ghost visitations, clouds, air, Emily Dickinson is in the room, fill in the blank.
(((((((	)))))))	=	other planets, kolob, space, major climactic or apocalyptic events.
(((o!)))		=	surprise, awe, yawn, praise, supplication, pleasure, pearl.
:::::::::::		=	stars, pearls, daisy chain, diadem, constellations, eggs, insects, microbes.

NOTES ON THE WRITING OF *The Lapidary's Nosegay*

I'm sitting with the (((P(o)etess))) in the (((chrysolite))) (((sun)))

((((   ))))

Well-cleaned (((glass))) sh(o)ws my (o)wn rocky garden

        n(ew)   zion   's   mountain—

(((emerald))) in spring   (((silver)))   summer sage

            autumnal   (((hyacinth))) (((amber)))   &

                  my (ow)n (((dry g(o)ld)))   &

slatey-white   ::::::::::::::   winter (((diamond))) mountains

        My ((gh(o)st))   &   (((Emily's Gh(o)st)))

                        fl(oa)t and waft thr(ough) f(ou)r seasons

(&)   I'm writing down her words ((((   ))))

                         (((She)))   patient

              teaches me the alphabet   of high desert   my deseret

& (((She)))   is :::

                ((((   ))))

        & has already engraven   &

the universe   (((((((   )))))))   it is long time finished :::::::

We are Calvin's bastard daughters—transl(u)cent heretics &

Christian women   seeded with invasive doctrines

My ((gh(o)st))

sees me as a weak-hybrid-housekeeper

a M(o)rmon Quakeress

(which is) practically (n(o)) thing at all

&

(((She)))

the ((Winged)) (((Queen))) of her (ow)n congregation of

b(o)ne &

(((flowers))) & (((j(ew)els))) & ((winged)) things

pr(o)fessing the herbarium   's   gospel

((((me thr(o)ugh the (((P(o)etess's wind(ow))))))))

(((o!)))

we lay down with (((god))) in our (ow)n dark l(oa)m

(((o!)))

we l(oa)med ourselves   with pre-eden's   ((gh(o)st))

((cherubim))   & (((fire))) ((((((()))))))

When did *optizan* become *optician*?

When did the optizan begin t(o) create little (((wind(ow)s)))

for our eyes   & what instr(u)ments did the optizan use

?

& how did he kn(ow) about the inside of the eye   & what t(o) d(o) next

?

& what does

(((Her)))   1844   N(o)ah Webster's dictionary[†]

say about the spellings   ?

How was their vision—a spectacle a pince-nez a ((((((mon(o))))cle)))

?

Did he pr(o)vide a chamois

f(o)r th(o)se wh(o)se vision he fixed

?

a cloth for (((shining))) up the (((glass)))

& clearing up the

(((vision)))

[†] *Emily read the dictionary "as a priest his breviary." The collected poems contain over 9,275 unique words and nearly 100,000 word occurrences.*

?

We ((heard))   that the P(o)etess was always

(((god)))

outfashioned

Retrieving odds and meters

from extant matter

& shaping miniscule stitchings & scratchings &

pressings—

scraps of linen just b(o)rdering legibility

Outfashioned—

never   outvisioned—

& all thr(ough)

four seasons   we ((gh(o)sts)) sit

We sit

Calvin's heretical

((gh(o)st))   daughter(s)

We sit   We waft   We are quiet breathers   &

we like t(o) be al(o)ne with (o)nly ((gh(o)sts))

&   we like t(o)

(((look thr(ough) wind(ow)s)))   & we like   (((things)))   and (((wings)))

& t(o) ask   & t(o) und(o)

what (((diamond))) tongue p(o)ets   did wrong

to redeem   their sin

((((   ))))

Gh(o)sts like words

that (((look))) like   (((flowers)))

& t(o) pray (((beneath bonnet brims))) in (((god's))) tent of temple trees

& thr(ough) (((shining))) (((glass wind(ow)s)))

t(o) pr(o)tect ourselves from th(o)se sharp (((diamond)))

tongues   trying to etch   our (((wind(ow)s)))

with worldy   heresy

wh(o) never engraved a letter on (((this onyx world))) or

a word on (((g(o)lden))) tablets

or ink on linen or stationer's scraps

never did this world reply

& t(o) make crooked things

(((o!)))

(((t(o) crook the straightened crooked path)))

& t(o) wear strands of thirty-one

(((pearls))) (o)ver the breast & beneath high collars

(((((((Pearl))))))) is

(((Her))) (((m(o)st))) gl(ow) & sound

((My)) (((gh(o)st)) a queer & quiet quakeress)

& (((Emily))) (((Gh(o)st)))

(((Daisy Wraith)))

(((Belle Flower)))

(((Butterfly)))

(((( ))))

THE LAPIDARY'S NOSEGAY

A

In Adam's fall

We sinned all

A sudden (((bright coin)))

turns in the sky

bringing (((vi(o)lets)))

from their furr(ow)s

*

girls eat plums on the p(o)rch

((winged ((gh(o)sts)) in sodden gowns)) water the sheep

call the (((lambs)))

& (((thren(o)dies of (((pearl)))

sung by a ((bird)))))

& grasses reft

the ash tree

the p(oo)r man's (((magnificent))) (((onyx))) lance breaks in a trice

the rich man's op(u)lent peril

*

our bodies

once sunken ref(u)se

are ((drawn)) from the earth ((her baggage a strapped (((pearl)))))

*

(((daff(o)dils)))   (((pansies)))

(((( ))))

amen

Ambuscade[†] of (((cl(o)ver)))

D(ew)'s viands

(((giddy bees))) consecrate

the droplets' caplets

*

breadths of ((pl(u)med)) mead(ow)s (((pasque flowers)))

rear thirsty ((butterflies)) in keen bonnets—

mesmeric enfranchised ((belles))

twine

(((supple c(o)teries of)))

((umber & gamb(o)ge lepidoptera)) (((P(o)et's))) c(ou)riers

(((all ambery shine)))

peep up beside the trudger's way—

meek (((bartsia)))— plush (((silvery))) lamb's ear

the bashful pilgrim that builded a (((stalactite))) chanticleer

& sleeps

under (((heaven's))) c(o)ld shroud :::

among sheaves & under the (((((multiplication of celestial j(ew)els)))))

---

† *"Dear Abiah, have you made you an herbarium yet? I hope you will if you have not, it would be such a treasure to you; most all the girls are making one"(Emily Dickinson, 1845).*

(((Angels))) babble—

((((::))))

a ((chorus of ruffled axioms & dandelion[†] baffle))

(&) their murmurs (((firmaments))) & clean (((glass)))

(&) angels tossing puzzles

(&) st(o)ne showers & (((pearls)))

(&) (((sapphires)))

thumping down beside our beds

*

in late summer

the fainting ((bee's)) dull (((stab)))

the scarlet ((bird's)) (((((ruby-thr(oa)ted))))) slash

the raffle of last (((blossoms)))

bl(ow)n against the fence

&

((my happy tamb(ou)rine))—

((scalds)) that summer's (((cincture)))—

int(o) evening's ((((o)pal diadem))) (((( ))))

[†] *Dandelion (Taraxacum): Smiling on all; coquetry (Ms. Almira H. Lincoln Phelps).*

*

my tongue

dumb murmurs

with thirst

the (((scarlet bird’s)))

embroidered

nest

B

Thy life t(o) mend,

(((((((God's))))))) Book attend

Beetle's (o)rdination

conferred ((a spelling)) & a lining out the patientest

of this congregation's season—

(((the ch(o)rister waves her b(o)ne)))

*

c(o)mbing leaves from her (((r(o)sy))) ringlets—

(((Daisy))) crumbles leaves int(o) her box

(((three birds plumb the sky)))

a squirrel and his nut cl(o)mbe the stile he h(oa)rded scraps of p(o)em for f(oo)d

*

amphritite's whim—

her blanched mien seamless—

breaching salty waves (((iridescent))) in a shell of

(((mother of))) (((pearl))) a storm gl(ow)ers

bleak— rem(o)ter—

against a sm(o)ky (((sky)))

we clam(o)r t(o) split ourselves before (((her)))

*

hammer's (((spark))) ((blank (&) leaden bl(ow)s))—

pebbles and ac(o)rns fly—

we joggle seasons together

Br(o)ken spectacles

crushed (((hyacinth)))[†] petal lenses

branches barred against the (((sky)))

rock—

(((sky)))—

branch—

slumber(eth)

[†] *Hyacinth (Hyacinth): Love is full of jealousy (Ms. Almira H. Lincoln Phelps).*

(((**B**uttercups)))   (((ranunculuses)))

(((pasque flower)))   (((anem(o)ne)))

(((hepatica))) retrimmed   in crimson heart-blood

&

idle bells ((((   ))))

(((exultantly garlanded)))

pledge to tipt(oe)

around sprigs   (our slippers)   of unpuzzled mosses

*

the (((birdling's)))   blithe   buttonh(o)le

& our hems & pinions tarnished   with heaven's   (((gem d(ew))))

by mead(ow)'s traverse

(((& chafed by amber august sun)))

*

trippingly adrift

bewildered

by ph(o)t(o)graphs of (((Our P(o)etess of Amherst Our (Ow)n Venus Genetrix)))

& her severely parted auburn hair & (((Thy))) dainty lips

((feel (((Her Lip))) as a ((hummingbird)) sipped just (((Me)))))

concealing (((Daisy's))) (((r(u)by))) teeth

C

The Cat doth play,

And after slay

Chartered from (((my otter's wind(ow))))—

&

the (((glazier))) has come and gone

his view t(o) mine ceded (((The Anch(o)ress's view)))

((((((o!))) juggler of glass)))

strung across the face of my d(o)mestite—

(n(ew) gl(o)be's (((glass))) vision)

(((( ))))

this shape of (((day))) & (((day))) & (((day))) (&)

strung out like (((j(ew)els)))

& packed

around a clasped chain of maidenh(oo)d's (((pearls)))

*

shamming ((((o)pals)))

dowered in (((chrys(o)lite)))

bending

t(o) the quenching pond

h(o)rses (maidens) (((The Wayward Nun))) (feigning h(o)meliness)

poise at their next pond sipping

(((past a yawning hill)))

(((o!)))

D

A Dog will bite

A Thief at Night

(((Daff(o)dils)))   (((my blondines)))

        work y(ou)r dirten bed

(((& y(ou)r little cups brimming)))—

& y(ou)r ermine soil—

      offering its viands

& the hock upon y(ou)r leaflets

*

(((o!))) species & genera of (((n(o)segay)))†

(((o!))) royal-blooded b(o)tanic dingle

(((o!))) product of broad gales and dim cradles

(((o!))) visions in hildegard's bed chamber—

((((   ))))

*

bef(o)re y(ou)r ruddy necr(o)mancy

i am a ((blank balladeer))

my pr(o)lix verses fade

† *Ms. Almira H. Lincoln Phelps recommends that you compile your own floral dictionary—following your own heart and sentiments.*

bef(o)re y(ou)r mitred & bustling (((bl(oo)m)))

(& s(o)) i come (&)

(i am at m(o)st)

(((a clement tr(ou)badour)))—

Declined (((day)))

        begins the envoy   (&)   phantom's bare (&) gr(o)ping feet—

        (((jarred stars in early twinkling)))—

y(ou)r secret an enterprise   & a trace of lesser (((m(oo)n)))

((   ))   (((   )))   ((((   ))))   (((((   )))))   ((((((   ))))))

        & she crept t(o) our d(oo)r—   (((m(oo)n)))

                ((rides like our ((Gh(o)st Girl)) thr(ough) t(o)paz))

        i measure y(ou) against my fist

*

        step int(o) the sh(oe) of (((m(o)rning)))

its staid s(o)le against the c(o)ld—

                arc of a (((day)))   creature—

ample as   the (((l(o)rd's))) scr(o)ll of days   ((eternity is ample))

                        ((((((((((((((((((((((((   ))))))))))))))))))))))))

Dim unsuspected tenderness

hands us a (((n(o)segay)))

(((((whispers)) gentians))) bl(ow)n in ((ears))

plucks (((petals))) warm wraps &

stitcheried (((r(o)settes)))—

& azure—

falling—

&—

(((( ))))

*

& on an errand of conjecture th(o)se (((p(o)sies))) have foll(ow)ed us here

t(o) the mead(ow)—

(((( ))))

(((where our vi(o)lets quaked in long (((chrys(o)lite))) grasses)))

we drear & sessile creatures

(((suff(u)sed with nectar & d(ew))))

taken by (((bl(oo)m)))

trampled by (((smile))) & (((perf(u)me)))   ((((   ))))

*

(((((o!)))   letter   s!!!))

Wheref(o)re   marauder   art   thou   here?
Because   sir   love   is   sweet.

((((((( )))))))

a (((sun)))[†]   sliding strains of s(o)lstice—

stalls & bends   mouthing   the vowels of the secret sounds

(&)   then   t(o) l(ow)er its head

(&) int(o) the coming   of (((Belle's))) g(oo)d (((day)))

---

† *Sunflower (Hellanthus): you are too ambitious (Ms. Almira H. Lincoln Phelps).*

E

The ((Eagle's)) flight

Is out of Sight

Eyes—   little (like) trees—

comely infant

(((with still pulsing fond)))

just beyond the veil—

(((seeding)))

between   worlds—

(&) whilst y(ou) were

cons(o)rting with   (((early bees)))

(&) then n(o)tified

that it was nearly time   on g(oo)d (((morrow)))   t(o)   ((speak))

babbled syllables   t(o) read   from   (((Her)))   j(ew)elled primer

F

The idle F(oo)l

Is whipt at Sch(oo)l

(((((**F**airy P(o)et)))))

(((she chalked ont(o) the sky)))— (((( ))))

c(o)chineal—

marj(o)ram—

(&) (((god's))) (((gem-tactics)))—

colors t(o) tease & slake ((flit))

& ((flit)) unannointed

until we put a ((word)) t(o) every insect—

*

espy the (((clouds)))

tatter & stitch & knit ragged fabric

int(o) kirtle apron (((god's))) garment & raiment

until (& they are gone)—

(((god))) shrives & shrives them

*

the creek recedes

(in alm(o)st (((j(u)ly))))

& each bare f(oo)t

(& each wilting)   (& each)

on its (ow)n pebble

desert in parch—

its creatures—happy grackling

not beguiled!   (((o!)))

(desiccated) little desert

*

(((Daisy!)))

crouch behind me (&)   next march   (((rain)))   will wade y(ou)r creek

dimple int(o)   (((yell(ow)lets)))   (((god)))   (((smiles)))

G

As runs the (((Glass))),

Man's life doth pass

((Gh(o)st)) (((bl(oo)ms)))

(o)ver autumntime

across the m(oa)t

((sh(oe)less plea))

((ransomed)) ((gaunt))

((aught in their pockets))

t(oo) (slight) & dumb for hearing—

*

(((harebell))) (&) (((jessamine)))

(((capering)))

thr(ough) the chamber of dumb-gh(o)sted ((winged)) ((august))—

(((tippling))) (((humming)))

their ((clocks))—

holl(ow) docile specters—

humbler & such softer ((ticks))—

sweep the mead(ow)s

(&) sc(oo)p out earth's last (((pearls)))

*

cl(oa)ks fall off

of (((harebell))) & (((jessamine)))

(&) slashes of yell(ow) & purple

make (((bright foils))) against dry dun

*

the mashed fields (((have sh(oo)ken down)))

sn(o)w outweighs the grasses

mon(o)tr(o)paunifl(o)ra(((indianpipe)))heli(o)tr(o)pi(u)marb(o)rescents(((heliotrope)))

in Daisy's collecting tin ready f(o)r pressing[†]

(arrange y(ou)rselves f(o)r winter)

[†] *"Dear Abiah, I'm going to send you a little geranium leaf in this letter, which you must press for me"(Emily Dickinson, 1845).*

(((**G**l(o)be)))—bashful—((humming))

—human frith

its (((spikenards))) undrained—

optizan's garden (((reddening)))— & this— ((( ))) ((((o)dor)))

has published & pollinated y(ou)r fate

*

raised (&)

(((leaping))) up (((lilac))) (((chyrs(o)beryl)))

& gowns be-gemmed & b(o)tanic ::: (((o!)))

seedlings' hidden teeth

feet of the earth walk int(o) (((spheres)))

(((Green artificer)))—

((lepidoptera)) c(ou)riering   (((chrys(o)beryl)))

l(o) bent ((angel))—   (((P(o)etess!))) ((moth-lofting))

(&)   butterfly nibbles my ((ear))

sublimer ((angel (((chrys(o)lite))) & P(o)etess))—

(&)   her lisp perplexes (((flowers)))

circassian (((blazing))) ((Angel Queen))—

(&)   she trifles

(&)   cunning(ly)

(which r(u)by's mine?)

i am worsted by her (((gem-tactic)))

i surrender

((((   ))))

H

My Book and (((Heart)))

Shall never part

(((H(oa)rd of (((gems))))))

the scarlet's clutch (&) *

the b(o)ne's maus(o)leum (&) *

the l(o)garithm's primer (&) *

dumb testifier's phosph(o)r

*

fractures int(o) ((wings))— our interview unskeined

& before that (((jeh(o)vah)))

*

the (((glass bl(o)wer))) fills the (((sky))) :::

the p(o)et's smocked nightgown her frock on the bed

a black eclipse

(((anthracite))) lies hidden

& w(o)n't (((burn))) the (((c(oa)ly))) night

::::::::::::::::::::::::::::::::

I

isaiah's (gh(o)st) guest

(&)

(((i))) write the palimpsest

(((**I**))) died

the (((girl god p(o)et))) of this (small canyon)

quaking leaves (((silver aspen)))

(((tiny obscure c(o)dexes)))—

i'm desiccated in (((lavish))) sod!

obvolved— —in our (((l(o)rd's))) linen shawl

ad(o)rned in (((his)))

(((shining trinkets)))

in his worms

in his small creatures

(((his))) (((( ))))) j(ew)els against my b(o)ne

this l(oa)my crested & grave cons(o)lation

((linnet))less & scarfless

against my ((wingless flutter))

fr(u)gal squirrel's browning nut in my teeth

& (((glee r(o)se)))

I gather idle (((bumblebees)))

& s(ew) (((cl(o)vers))) int(o) a tarnished (((yell(ow))))   (((   )))   summer frock—

it is t(oo)   (((hot)))   f(o)r quaint tranquility

*

when (((buttercups))) (((beam blithe)))   across the field's periphrasis

((listen)) f(o)r fall

f(o)r ((how still))   the landscape h(o)lds f(o)r its p(o)rtrait

f(o)r ((how nonchalant)) the w(oo)d

& f(o)r where ((mosses have b(o)rne up))—

(((auburn m(o)rning)))

*

(((the h(o)rizon's b(o)rder chafes)))

sprigs & (((pearls))) line & entender

the ((whip(oo)rwill's)) ((((jacinth)))) nest

J

J(o)b feels the Rod,

Yet blesses (((god)))

Jointed—

(((o!))) (((pyrite stars)))—

with my (((shr(ew)der needle)))

garnered & stitched int(o)

(((o!))) n(o)teless evening

int(o) summer's noiseless ((gh(o)st)) raiment

& y(ou)r incautious ((gh(o)st)) cover—

& the zephyrless dark—

(((day's sky)))

*

sm(oo)thed

bef(o)re evening's brow withdr(ew)

& (o)'ert(oo)k my (((heart))) f(o)r birds &

modest viands f(o)r (((Our Tiny P(o)et)))

& (((constellations))) (((sh(o)ne))) thr(ough) this (((wind(ow))))

& ((rapt)) enrapture (((( )))) &

(((( ))))

*

& every pebble's affliction

(((savi(o)r)))

that barest

trodden by earth's feet

& (((ampler))) than (((cloud)))

K

Proud Korah's troop

Was swallow'd up

King's rep(o)se

(((( ))))

(((another bite!!! metallic sterling tongue & king's f(o)rk & tines)))

prithee t(o) drowse

in our bonnie bonnie (((plush))) & bonnie

holl(ow)

sp(oo)ning & retreat

drowsy (((gl(o)w))) twisting &

stringing our locks of hair t(o)gether

& (((glass))) leaflets

& (((p(o)rcelain))) berries—

fitted and seamed

int(o) our c(o)ve (((a moment!)))

(((((a grey dove c(oo))))))

(((( ))))

(((o!))) manuscript of (((love)))— vine of (((jessamine)))[†]

where n(o!) one fumbled

[†] *Samuel Bowles, who called Emily "daisy" and "queen," gave her a jasmine vine she kept alive for decades. In her herbarium, Emily writes of jasmine, "you are the soul of my soul." To Emily the jasmine meant passion.*

n(o!) one sc(o)rned

n(o!) one drammed us t(o) sleep—

the pods br(o)ke—

& (((o!!!)))

((((   ))))

((d(o) not turn the page))

L

The Lion bold

The Lamb doth hold

Lost—

her hagiography was nearly not found

—thank lavinia f(o)r rummaging thr(ough) her chest of drawers

retrieving the scraps the hand-s(ew)n fascicles

the flaps & strips and scratched revelations

*

stolid ((bee)) stitching nectar

(((worsting knotting knitted)))

int(o) (((purpling flowers)))

& accedes hexagonal t(o)

a pr(u)dent & fertile (((chamber)))

c(o)mb & hexagon pistil & stamen

((((((o!))) nectar)))

a st(o)ne lives again

t(o)ld our ((bee)) brother

to r(o)ll

thr(ough) field & ((wing)) again

M

The Moon gives light

In Time of Night

My

   &   (((Her)))

         (((Our Daylily P(o)etess))) (((parasols))) falling—

      off our b(oo)k's† illegible branches

                  inky

                    (((frilling & parach(u)ting)))

   to where n(e)w b(o)nes gr(o)w

in dirten graves

   pl(u)mes prest & shivered

      sipping the soil

   past-ripened burrs & ((gh(o)st)) berries

      b(o)ne branches   ((gh(o)st pallor))

            as if

      (((quartz))) whitened

(under?) (against?) (from?)

            (the sky?)

*

---

† *"How could we have ever doubted these?" he cried.* (*Thomas W. Higginson as cited in* White Heat: The Friendship of Emily Dickinson and Thomas Wentworth Higginson).

(((Moth-star dropt)))   int(o) the (o)rchard

and last night—

(((o!)))

the wind has already been ((murmuring))

(((o!)))

int(o) the petite ear

of the (((asph(o)del)))—stilly—

& sealed with green (((gentian)))   nectar

smuggled int(o) the demijohn

*

girt & epauletted summer stands

(o)verseasoned & (o)verdrest for fall—

the stand of treble-throated ((sparr(ow)s)) threads

the (((amethyst))) needle thr(ough)

one season's (((eye))) & int(o) the next &

robs the housewife of a day's (((bl(oo)m)))

her (((wind(ow)s))) wiped   &   polished t(o) naught

(((& vanished!)))

the (((p(o)et's))) erasure

((the entire alphabet wings int(o) her nest))

& a ((spotted bird)) suddenly reads

(((god's))) n(ew) primer

N

Nightingales sing

In Time of Spring

Night (((onyx)))

& (((diamond))) :::

& a sh(oo)t pushes from its bulb

& in her thr(oe)s she (((unf(o)lds)))

& sunders the earth ((( )))

—that wends three ways— ((( ))) (((( )))) ((((( )))))

*

tree b(o)nes & ((gh(o)st)) steeples

& modest little ((birds)) wh(o)se ((wings)) they st(o)le from

(((Daisy!)))

(((th(o)se naughty deb(au)chees)))

(((wh(o)se capers))) we can never attend

in that little brake & str(o)ll t(oo) far t(o) cross

from (((Daisy's))) thresh(o)ld

& her father's lawn

*

((linnet bird)) makes us little ::::::::

& his solemn bar(o)nial thrust of chest

        & his little laugh   brother treble

& y(ou)r pr(o)file passing thr(ough) my wind(ow)

                (while (((Daisy!))) is rapt in a curtain)

& y(ou)r thoughtsome blink & elegy

        t(o) my day's (((eye)))

        misspent little (((star)))

        ((bird))   ((sing))

                f(o)r my   (((Belle P(o)et)))

O

The royal Oak, it was the Tree

That sav'd his royal Majesty

(((**O!**)))   (((heart)))-sodden!!!

beggared   &   bewildered

at the (((diadems)))

y(ou) counted (((crescents)))

on (((m(o)rning's))) mountains

&   on arcs   on strings of (((onyx))) beads

on (((pearls))) dotted & dotted   around the d(oo)r of the lady chapel

*

& the evangelist surrenders—his s(o)rest (((heart))) bursts

(((r(u)bystone heartbl(oo)d)))

& ((wings))   & she ((clears)) the rafters

(and his ark was (((lit)))   with   a single great (((r(u)by))))

*

our (((hearts))) are discover'd

sc(oo)ped out of their cavities

& (((meek jesus's))) (((garnet))) bl(oo)d

running thr(ough) our pipes

Our (((august))) antiquary ransacks &

solders us int(o) fall—

heedless fr(o)m season

(((t(o) season))) ((the cl(o)se of nature's party))

while guiltless (((buttercups))) nod ranunculuses on the (((P(o)etess's))) lea

*

((had (((He))) seen (((Daisy's!))) season

(((god))) would think

(((His))) paradise s(u)perfl(u)ous))

*

(((Daisy's))) dropping seed ((whispers))

import(u)ning the granite diagram

of winter—

& the bernardine c(o)ld that

scalds our breath int(o) (((bl(oo)m)))

hasps fasten shut

the pane t(o) summer

(((Daisy petals))) sigh

*

(((Belle's))) s(o)rcery

(((dizzy!!!)))   with scribing

        (((Her))) n(ew)-fashioned day

& pouting august   (ind(o)lent   not ((listening)) t(o) (((Daisy))))

        straggles behind

the tongue's frail (o)rders

                                        (((winn(ow))))

        winn(ow)   &

bl(ow) the chaff   :::

P

Peter denies

His Lord, and cries

Pare this sapphire (((apple)))

of s(u)percilious bl(ue)

& b(o)lts of uns(ew)n watered silk

lodged in (((Great Aunt's))) box (o)f fascicles—

& wrapt around garnet br(oo)ches and sleeve buttons

f(o)reign (((corals))) & came(o)s

((but (((Daisy))) never wears j(ew)els))

(((i))) conceal (((Her))) suffering within a stanza's grey

calyx (o)r beside a ((h(oo)ting owl))

*

(((god's))) pier peeps (((out int(o) the emerald (o)cean)))

that unscr(o)lled wraith of salty br(o)cade

licks its prodigious will &

h(o)rrid tongue against the (((Glittering Dowerless Girl)))

wh(o)m (((god))) & the ((((o)cean))) had never met

& then

the Tide

Went past my simple Shoe—

And past my Apron—and my Belt

And past my Boddice—too—

And made as He would eat me up—

As wholly as Dew

*

(((of))) our n(ew) (((pearl))) bodies

::: afford our waves and their washings

*

And He—[(o)cean]—He followed—close behind—

I felt His Silver Heel

Upon my Ancle—Then My Shoes

Would overflow with Pearl—

Pauper's slit of silk

& g(o)lden thread

(((She))) wanted (((g(o)ld))) lathings

(((She))) got (((dove))) grey gloves

        &

etchings notched in the sparse twig of the insect's leg—

            thin enough to thread a pauper's needle—

even the tiny gnat—the miniaturest of (((god's))) (((gems)))

(((a midge's thimble of beggary)))—

                —lisped litanies   & lists drowned by th(o)se sharp (((diamond)))

                                      tongues wh(o)

                              silenced (((Daisy))) in a cedar chest

                the cilium in y(ou)r left ((ear)) felt her breath m(o)ve their fringes

*

then—daff(o)dil   swerveless

bef(o)re all creatures &

        y(ou)r blistering—

J(o)b's costly (((r(u)by))) carbuncles

        & b(oo)tless cries—

tossing yell(ow) gems from (((Her))) s(o)res—

        int(o) the vexed and twining wind—

The (((**P**(o)et's))) zephyr angry

that her (((j(ew)el)))—encrusted harp cannot be heard

even with the perf(u)med gale of

(((His))) magnificent (((floral breath)))

*

(((Our Neglected Lady)))

(((Her))) wizardry & bright declaimings

outvisioning & outranking cr(u)cifixal rank

*

maddest (((diamond))) scratchings on vellum

declaimings lathings—

the antel(o)pe's quick wizardry

(((The Antel(o)pe P(o)et

(((She))) runs but she cannot jump the (((Pearly fence)))

& needs some (((god))) to lift (((Her))) (o)ver

the etchings of (((Her))) (((diamond)))-tongued predat(o)r)))

her (((onyx))) alphabet is engraven & (((parceled))) in yell(ow) t(u)lle—

your ((prayer)) a cedar chest of p(o)ems ajar—

& bulbs dropped

into l(oa)my furrows t(oo) early in spring—

&

(((o!)))   ringing in my b(o)nes

lighted wind(ow)s

—(((sh(o)ne))) & sounded from every evening—

*

suddenly unbraided stretch of agate r(oa)d   (o)ver machine-stitched bl(u)e felt hills—

even minor (((stars))) adequate ((swinging their cups of (((chrys(o)lite))) goblet))

& sn(ow)flaked diamonds—

the chill r(oa)ms beside me

glad for (((god's))) infinity   as it ever were

(& and &)

(((Daisy's Gh(o)st))) is here

Peeps ont(o) that sleeping (((egg))) (((   )))

(((Our Lady's virgin (((pearl))))))

eclipses ((my)) frittered day

the ditties   &

the crumbs   &   the toddled hours

(((((Daisy's))) days turn t(o) t(o)paz like a lady's pin))

& my tired (((r(u)by heart))) that (((She))) s(oo)thed into her (((pearl basket)))

sc(oo)ping herbarium's an(o)dyne

ont(o) my parched tongue

(((&)))

(((   )))

*

sleep &   (((c(oo)))) like ((Daisy's D(o)ve))

t(o) w(oo)

&   —sleep—

while a   (((molten)))

((((   ))))

m(oo)n is (((watching)))

Q

Queen Esther comes in royal State,

To save the Jews from dismal Fate

Quivering—

(((o!)))   (((op(u)lent))) (((Queen of Heaven)))

((while we play at paste

till qualified f(o)r (((pearl)))))

—& gossamer—

stilly starry

showers of (((pearls))) :::::::::::::

(((   )))

int(o)   jumbled gushing   midnight

::::::::

::::::::

::::::::

::::::::   ....

::::::::

R

Rachael doth mourn

For her first-born

Ragged phoebes (((trem(o)r))) :::

where is the (((g(o)ld?))) the dimity

& the (((bullion)))

(((& the beryl?))) (((&))) where the (((maize?)))

a prophet's finger touching (((r(u)by)))

under veils of cobweb (((the m(o)st precious thread in (((Her))) s(ew)ing box)))

& pods & glistenings & droplets & (((o!)))

(((icicles))) are

(((l(o)rdly sardonyx & scimitars)))

*

intoxicating & filamental (((godly))) gifts

flying down the aisles of winter

green grave turning white—

(((chrys(o)lite))) t(o) (((crystal)))

& glistening

& glistening

in (((god's))) sweet clay creases

((Rapt)) (((::::: m(o)rning of all m(o)rnings)))

& apricots

on the (((bramble)))

& a spilled box of (((pearls)))

& trees vassals of the ill-kempt l(o)nely lane

branches (((undressing))) from their fr(ui)ts

& r(o)sy (((gleaming))) bef(o)re each rare & ad(o)red pedestrian

*

(((Our Mother))) is a (((dot of accidental ink on the man(u)script)))

(((A Pressed Petal))) between our pages.

((((She))) doth flutter

on the h(o)rizon)

*

(((o!))) my hidden n(oo)k on the hill

& (((o!))) how beautiful upon the mountain

(are Thy feet) (rapt) (hurtling) (disc(o)rdant)

how sweet & changeable thy quaintly flinging gl(oa)ming garments

(((gl(oa)m)))

R(ou)ge—

& the (((lisp))) of last crepe

crimson on the branch

of n(o)vember dissolves

& f(o)restalls

(((blazed))) int(o) december

(((pleas))) that (((P(o)etess))) had already

puzzled out before we even kn(ew) her

*

(((o!))) (((god!)))

fetch us that (((timid))) apron of sn(o)w

firmamental in the d(o)ting (((sun)))—

& the broad cuff of trees

where spurned ((birds)) hide (((blaze))) & perch

*

winter ((night phosph(o)resces))

& climbs int(o) bed & mangles & plies her

& the sky-punctures

& dapples

& flinging light & clouds

:::: & ::::
:::: & ::::
:::: & ::::

S

Samuel anoints

Whom God appoints

September's escutcheon

(espies)

the preparations of her vestments—

we inhale the (((parched)))

((gust)) of august—

the ((gh(o)st breath)) & the h(o)ly shard of (((Spirit)))

wrapt in gauze (((sun)))

hiding her nimble incisions—

while (((god's gh(o)st stitcher—Daisy—s(ew)s s(o) prettily)))

winter's surplice—& spring's kirtle—

filling (((god's))) meager winter tr(ou)ss(eau)   with skirts and petals

*

then we kn(o)w fall's ruddy scrabble

(will end in b(o)ne)

& sl(ew)n tattered dandelions   their fluff flung int(o) (((Daisy's))) pearl basket

(((flower))) stems lying in dark parl(o)rs

for the necr(o)mancer's

unnumbered alms

(the dandelion's baffled pall

long scattered)

(((o!))) struggling rill (((o!))) stilled & songless rill

the final amethyst will not be ushered in

(((Sn(ow))))   aprilly does (((Gh(o)st))) & whiff across the altar

in that (first) of gardens

(((& slakes))) h(o)liness &

the holl(ow)ness

of springtime

&

(((Emily's))) (((blossom))) daughters shiver

in (((sun)))dresses

& (((glass))) bleeds

at the sn(ow)flakes' incisions

& the winter

sketches st(o)rms on the wind(ow)

& everyone is scarred &

eating their (ow)n ((wings)) in desperation

&

mar(oo)ned in his t(o)mb   (sleeping & sleeping) (((jesus)))

&

i have emptied pearls from oyster shells & clamped empty shells ont(o) my shoulder blades replacing the ((wings)) (((i ate)))

&

the empty r(o)sebush   &   the greening th(o)rny poignards

i select a (((glass))) st(o)ne to r(o)ll in each hand

& (((o!)))nly a tailor's pick t(o) uns(u)ture (((my skull))) & (o)pen

just enough t(o) fly

a sterling teasp(oo)n of millet

t(o) (((god's))) unh(o)ly page

T

Time cuts down all,

Both great and small

The child is scr(o)lled up like a small pretty ((ear))

(dropped!) (((o!)))

on an unr(o)lled lawn— of dark emerald j(ew)eler's felt

& that little wrecked (((emperor)))

(abashed!!!)

& under aftern(oo)n's heft

import(u)ning the robin (in the grass)

to take a crumb

from his marked (o)pen palm

*

(((child)))—slim with thin feathers

hunched against the firmament's j(ew)el cloth—

seal y(ou)r breath in y(ou)r beak

upon the ((bird's)) deep plunge

int(o) the pond (((you are not a bird!)))

(((&))) (((o!)))

how plashless on the water!

*

& yet

will the melting sn(o)w

numb our chilled dangling fingers—treading

(((thr(ough)))) the ample season's stream

& (((o!)))

it will be days

((his valves (o)pen and shut on (((r(u)by))) (((heart's))) blood))

till we kn(o)w if he will ((rise))

the child's eyelids pink (((r(o)se petals)))

(((o!))) if (o)nly (((god))) would break the seal

(((Timbral))) she fleshly flickers—

&

autumn's epicures

dip down &

wash down to sin(ew)—

whilst ::::::::

*

((birds)) have flitted from the brake

r(u)bies t(o)paz unr(o)lled from green felt

& then put back in the dirt—

& dull darkle gives way (to blot)

*

drill int(o) their gilded sepulchres

sublimer courtiers

than their couriers in hiding

&

y(ou)r cease (&) fretting—

the ((P(o)et Bird)) & her clever per(u)ke   & her c(oa)ly eye   hath hindered winter

:::

—they have notched the trees beneath your lit wind(ow)

        with their hard diamond tongues—

    they are gone &

        the p(o)ets :::

they will never say y(ou)r alphabet

This (((broily))) day

—slides t(o) (((crepusc(u)le)))

& we wait for adamantine (((clouds))) t(o) spar

t(o) wreck & (o)pen

the vowels (that) dram our garden int(o) bl(oo)m

*

haply this day (((o!)))

we discovered the (((foxglove)))†

bef(o)re (((our))) small guest

had wandered out—

you espied its purple flamb(eaux)

i dug it out & kenneled

its

thimble of poison of (((o!)))

of deathly beautiful amethyst (((r(o)e)))

*

(((o!))) such seldom & transient glimmers

---

† *Foxglove (Digitalis): I am not ambitious for myself, but for you (Ms. Almira H. Lincoln Phelps).*

s(o) (((o!)))

(at clock's announcement)

wrap us in y(ou)r black mechlin laces

((sweet dram))   sweet deadly tincture

seal y(ou)r (((pearls)))   ont(o) a br(oo)ch

pin y(ou)r ((((o)pal))) t(o)   my   ((m(o)saic)) (((heart)))

Throng of ac(o)rns ::::::

& f(o)rest's eggs ((( )))

& (o)rchards (((ashine))) with apples ((( )))

each fr(ui)t bitten by the jasper teeth of the ((h(o)ly gh(o)st))

many c(u)bited c(ou)rsers ride

y(ou) t(o)wards fall

beclouded & less c(o)rdial

farewell halcyon fields from

(((god's m(o)st s(u)perfl(u)ous spillage of days)))

((((o)pened pods of peas)))

(the lapidary raised a hammer

above the peach st(o)ne—the last

diamond tumbled out—he declaims

the gem b(ou)quet—i'd f(o)rgotten he

had such a voice—purely (o)rnamental—

& such j(ew)el fever—)

u

Uriah's beauteous wife

Made David seek his life

((Unfrequented))   august

&   september's plunder

          (((apple   peach   &   pear)))

                    (((o!)))   the winey grapes from emerson's vine

          as we are shaping the end days int(o)   (((ingots)))

                                        &   january's flask

                    of (((gentian))) liquor beckons us

                              (((here—the gh(o)st whispers—here!)))

                                        (((Gentle Gh(o)st   Fierce P(o)etess)))

m(o)ldered field   feast laid on the f(u)neral table

          chid by the ((linnet's))   perfidy   (& her mon(o)phonic chants)

&   her capers   as   she flees your hillocks

she kn(ow)s

                    you kn(ow)

                                        she g(o)es   &

then venus bisects her pearl int(o) tw(o) magnificent eardrops

for y(ou) t(o) clip   t(o)   the   (((P(o)etess's)))

                                                  small virgin l(o)bes

(((pearls))) big as (((cle(o)patra's))) earbobs

& fastened under the temple of

(((Emily's))) soft white ((gh(o)st bonnet))

the (((gems)))

the tribes

a dozen months

twelve (((g(o)ld))) oxen

wrapt 'round a year's distaff

*

the carmine rent on her breast is covered

in straw & summer herbs

a n(ew)born lamb delivers

(((the chrys(o)lite))) he carries

in his sweet little mouth

breathing (((vi(o)let))) scented (((god))) breath

*

(((The P(o)etess))) lays out a scr(o)ll on the grass

the lamb licks off the seal the angels pr(o)claim (((Her)))

th(ough) she be in heaven already

::::::::::::::::::

V

We & victors all

ghosts

god's quiet pall

Vane turns—

((((   ))))

—

—

—

((((   ))))

&   zephyret

of mazarine (((bliss)))

(((o!)))

(scant gems)

(bl(oo)dless cloud)

*

(((o!))) ample purchaser of w(o)rd & w(o)rld   (o) (clamberer)—

buy the gnat   her (ow)n single day

man and midge ::::::::::   the mosquit(o)'s quiet breath

*

(((O!))) (Seamstress)

stitching tinted phrases of m(o)rning   ont(o) linen

fling aside y(ou)r wrapper

& unshroud y(ou)r (((shining glass)))

& reveille

f(o)r the (((lord's))) trumpeters can't hear :::

prop (((Daisy's))) d(oo)r ajar

th(ough) she be already a ((gh(o)st)) in heaven

W

Whales in the Sea

God's Voice obey

We have slendered ourselves

& all thr(ough) winter—

our mouths watered for a b(ow)l of ramp & rain

puddles of (((glass)))

& star shards in (((buttercuplets))) & ac(o)rn caplets

the coming of millennial quench of (((j(ew)els))) ::

*

(*harpist thrum :::   ((wings)) across the lyre

*beaks (o)pen :::   chant the (((salve (((Regina))))))   (((((   )))))

*purple songlet) :::

*

wages (were never) earned ::: paid at season's turn?

which we dr(ew) in the slatey & flinty way of clay men

all thr(ough) th(o)se many blanketless nights

wrapt in (((god's)))   c(o)ld air

*

we have swept ash

from our chimney skins

we have drummed poppyseeds from trees

while our b(o)nes (o)pen & shut :::

our (o)pen b(o)nes are d(oo)rs f(o)r s(oo)ty gh(o)sts t(o) enter :::

the rem(o)ter century still does not appr(oa)ch

*

y(ou)r (((lantern))) d(oo)r slips &

(((shines))) int(o) the niches b(o)red int(o) rocks

apocalypses p(ou)r acid from b(ow)ls

(((int(o)))) our (((concrete))) shelters

and even still

(((Her P(o)ems))) are etched & archived

int(o) (((god's))) granite

(((**W**ind(ow)'s))) (((sparkling))) an(o)dyne

does not fail—

(((Housewife P(o)et))) r(o)lling (Her)selves up in luscious b(o)lts of silk

secret scarlet skeins

that the spider friends

from the garden

fashioned f(o)r (((Her))) last day on this our (ow)n earth

a heart-blood red

r(u)by pill(ow)

(stuffed with downy spider silks)

d(ew)s f(o)r the (((P(o)etess's Head))) rest

f(o)r (((Belle's))) horrid slip int(o) unskeined tangle

a casket keepsake is the world's dumb gift

(((&)))

the needless heed & worship of failure

((((   ))))   (((o!)))

garden ((gh(o)sts)) kn(ow) of lists buried here and there

& stumbling decid(u)ous page marks

of flecks falling in between b(oo)k leaves :::

s(oo)n the alphabet falls & falls &

i am wrung

i am hiding in the eaves &

i

am

straightway

delirious

circumabulating

the stark goblet—

dropping spider starry down

::::::::::::::::::::

X

Xerxes the Great did die,

And so must you and I

(((ony**X**))) night :::::::::::::

brought e**X**tacy! the (((Singer's))) crown

& her ((gh(o)st)) diadem

& her ((gh(o)st girl))

wh(o) removed the te**X**tile she had stitched

::: crosses :::

f(o)rmed with her (ow)n ((gh(o)st)) hand

::: the (((jesus))) mark laid on its side

f(o)r ladies t(o) s(ew) in (((jesus l(o)rd savior's))) (ow)n le**X**icon :::

(((the l(o)rd's))) (ow)n phosph(o)rescent n(o)segay

filled with lapidary's bl(((oo)))ms

(((buttercup))) (((sardony**X**))) (((r(o)se))) & (((jessamine)))

(((gentian))) (((geranium))) (((indian pipe)))

(((day lily))) (((pasque flower)))

stitched with th(o)se stubborn auburn threads plucked from (((Daisy's Head)))

:::::::::::::::

& while (((Daisy's))) fascicles were stitching

their (ow)n escape

cottoned in chrysalis's embrace ::: in

butterfly's w(o)mb

they were merely

(((not e**X**actly)))

not breathing & not sleeping

the h(o)rridly certain ((((sleep))))

in trouss(eau)'s t(o)mb

but winging the (((Queen)))

in her (((chrys(o)lite))) casket my demure (((green-apple gem)))

((gh(o)st)) said (((( ))))

& her light was like a (((jasper))) st(o)ne a (((crystal)))

&

i stitched her in cart-wheeled (((**X**s))) across my bodice

& i used her gem-tactics

t(o) write my (ow)n beginning & end

what was herbarium's prophecy— ::: ???

Y

Youth forward slips,

Death soonest nips

(((Yclept))) & (((chrysalid)))

th(o)rny (((r(o)sy)))   (((r(u)by)))

thirty-one (((daisies)))

(o)pen t(o) thirty-one pearls

(((god)))

((o))pens his mouth t(o)

receive them thirty-one times

(((&)))

the (((P(o)et's))) crystal breastplate

be-gemmed†   (((&)))

unblushingly battle-raged from the world's silence

breath & wind of

*

the r(o)sier   the rust

the red   the (((beryl)))

the (((chrys(o)lite)))

*

---

† *"If the percentage of jewel words in the total wordage of the individual poets were to be compared, she would appear even more begemmed than such lapidaries as Browning and Tennyson" (Rebecca Patterson, "Emily Dickinson's Jewel Imagery").*

(((chrys(o)prase p(o)sies)))

(((&)))

& ((gh(o)st)) phosph(o)r

(((o!))) how the gh(o)st cuts flowers with her (((amethyst))) knife

& (((o!))) how

(((garnetly))) (bleeds the ancient carbuncle)

(((gushes))) the carmine

astounding tumbler of (((j(ew)el))) incidence

spilling from (((Our Lady's))) ebon brake :::::::

Z

Zaccheus, he

Did climb the Tree

His Lord to see

Zinnia???

(((o!)))—

n(o)—

not wilding enough

she is t(o)paz

the world's cipher[†]

hung from a diminutive g(o)lden chain

f(o)r (((Demure Daisy)))—

(wh(o) ref(u)ses j(ew)els)

*

the zer(o) & the zed of 1863

spider-wrap wrapt 'round (((T(o)paz)))

in a shroud of (((air))) as warm as a cloud ::::::

(((no))) petals enr(o)bing

our child-sized (((Daisy Queen)))

she's obvolved in

((n(o)!)) thing!!!

---

† *"And yet I know not why I feel that the world holds a predominant place in my affections"(Emily Dickinson, 1846).*

*

the carmine embroidery floss

threaded thr(ough) a wide-eyed needle   binds her linen pages

& tells us

((((   ))))

of what we thought we wanted to kn(ow)

*

th(o)se alphabets stitched

in her (((day lily))) diary

the primer she made

from what (((gh(o)sts))) & flowers

put in her ((ear))

which was this ::::::

((((   ))))

all the alphabet was already there

(((all—yes—all!!!)))

& all

the be-gemmed and bedecked prophets

desired t(o) meet her

when the butterfly c(ou)riered her unweighted b(o)nes & branches t(o) heaven

& they thought they might have

heard her speaking from her dark hallway—

*

& even the (((l(o)rd god himself))) made her a n(o)segay clear as glass

transparent as zer(o) :::

& even th(ough)

the world (that (o)ld nothing)

sent her an empty onion skin[†]—trif(o)lded &

(o)pening breathy & blank as stationery can be

she received ((n(o))) transl(u)cent thing in reply—

shake the empty envel(o)pe

—n(o) word scratch n(o) spider track n(o) address

n(o) snail has crossed the leaf—

*

the envel(o)pe

wax sealed & portending

good n(ew)s

† *"Do write me soon Dear A and let it be a long, long letter. Don't forget—!!!!! Your aff. friend, Emily ED" (Emily Dickinson, 1846).*

(((o!)))   (((o!)))   n(o)

(((her gl(u)ed & f(o)lded little coffin)))

*

when (((P(o)et Lamb)))

br(o)ke the seal   it ushered in

((((   ))))

*

when n(o) one wr(o)te back

we kn(ew) the p(o)ets

had apostatized

*

save the (((P(o)etess's))) (((ow)))n inky thumbprint

on that spinning glass gl(o)be world

it was g(o)ing t(o) wild away anyway

world—

:::   enough!

we kn(ow) all things

& n(o)   things   ((((   ))))

at all

(((In the name of the Bee—

And of the (((Butterfly)))

And of the Breeze—Amen!)))

(   ) + ((   )) = (((   )))
oh or *oo* sound or non-essential clause **PLUS** listen, ears, wings, angels, birds, butterflies, ghosts with or without wings, any other winged creature or the Belle of Amherst is speaking **EQUALS** petals, sun, pleasure, god, radiance, shine, gems.

(((   ))) + ((((   )))) = ((((((   ))))))
petals, sun, pleasure, god, radiance, shine, gems **PLUS** unsaid, unanswered, ineffable, prayer, the Holy Spirit, ghost visitations, clouds, air, Emily Dickinson is in the room, fill in the blank **EQUALS** other planets, kolob, space, major climactic or apocalyptic events.

(((o!))) + ( ) + (( )) + (((   ))) + ((((   )))) = (((((((((((((o!)))))))))))))
surprise, awe, yawn, praise, supplication, pleasure, pearl **PLUS** *oh* or *oo* sound or non-essential clause **PLUS** listen, ears, wings, angels, birds, butterflies, ghosts with or without wings, any other winged creature or the Belle of Amherst is speaking **PLUS** petals, sun, pleasure, god, radiance, shine, gems **PLUS** unsaid, unanswered, ineffable, prayer, the Holy Spirit, ghost visitations, clouds, air, Emily Dickinson is in the room, fill in the blank **EQUALS** the feminine first person singular pronoun.

ACKNOWLEDGMENTS

"Ragged phoebes ((tremor))" first appeared in *Gloom Cupboard*.

"(((H(oa)rd of (((gems)))))),"
"(((Globe)))—bashful—((humming)),"
"Beetle's (o)rdination," and "(((Timbral))) she fleshly flickers—" first appeared in *FRiGG*.

"((Gh(o)st)) (((bl(oo)ms))),"
first appeared in *Poets for Living Waters*.

"(((Daff(o)dils))) my (((blondines)))" first appeared in the *Crab Creek Review*.

"Ambuscade of (((cl(o)ver))),"
"(((Angels))) babble—,"
"Br(o)ken spectacles,"
"Dim unsuspected tenderness," and "(((((Fairy P(o)et))))),"
first appeared in *Bone Bouquet*.

"Pare this sapphire (((apple))),"
"Pauper's slit of silk,"
"The (((P(o)et's))) zephyr angry,"
"Peeps ont(o) that sleeping (((egg))) ((( ))),"
"Quivering—", first appeared in *Interim: a Journal of Poetry and Poetics*.

"(((Yclept))) & (((chrysalid))),"
first appeared in *Ocean State Review*.

"(((onyX))) night ::::::::::::::" and "Zinnia???" first appeared in *Abstract Magazine*.

With much gratitude and love for Donald Revell, who has long championed my work and poems, and this book specifically, and who showed me how to sustain life & poems in the middle of it all. I'm especially thankful for the generosity shown by Jacqueline Osherow, who was so giving of her time and her incredibly smart attention, and who helped me listen to my lines with better ears. With much thanks to the Taft-Nicholson Center and the Lawrence T. and Janet T. Dee Foundation for their support. Without the residency they provided in Centennial Valley, Montana, this book could not exist. It was such a joy and revelation to work with the staff and the interns of the Center for Literary Publishing. Kristin Macintyre's intelligence and insight was a gift, and at times epiphanic—I enjoyed every minute of work I did with her. Marie Turner's beautiful and carefully researched herbarium image could not have been more perfectly beautiful for the face of my book, and Christa Shively and Chelsea Hansen's detailed work on this challenging manuscript far exceeded my expectations. Stephanie G'Schwind is a pro with such a gracious touch—there is no question that this manuscript would not have come to fruition without her guidance and expertise. I know that this book presented many technical quirks and challenges quite outside the norm of most book production endeavors, and so wish to express an extra measure of thanks to the whole staff of the CLP. Many thanks to Jonathan Landry for the kind gift of his time and talent. I am obliged to so many readers, colleagues, teachers, friends, and family: Paisley Rekdal,

Katherine Coles, Marjorie Perloff, Craig Dworkin, Susan Griffin, and Jean Valentine; with thanks and remembrances for two late and most generous artists and teachers: Thomas Lux and Robert Ashley. Thanks to Janet McAdams, JL Jacobs, Yun Wang, Julie Nichols, Nathan Hauke, Derek Henderson, Susan Goslee, Jenny Colville, Erin Menut, Dian Monson, Marni Asplund Campbell, Susan Jacobowitz, and Julie Turley; to Joel Long, Brian Kubarycz, David Veloz, Michael McLane, and Michael Lee.

Thank you to the editors of *Abstract Magazine* for nominating "(((onyX))) night ::::::::::::::" for a Pushcart Prize.

I acknowledge my overwhelming good fortune in finding a new sweet home, and in this home, much repose; for the blessing and companionship of six incredible siblings; for the grace and joy given to me by my five beloved children, who are loved beyond love; for my always inspiring and heroic grandmothers, foremothers, and aunts; for my father, with his quiet, consistent encouragement and support; and most of all, for my mother, Wendy Ann Whitaker Candland, who put poetry inside me before I could speak, and who provided material and emotional sustenance for my life and for the lives of so many others with unstinting generosity.

And Daisy. Dear Beloved Daisy: thank you for the nosegay.

This book is set in Perpetua
by The Center for Literary Publishing
at Colorado State University.

Copyediting by Kristin Macintyre.
Proofreading by Christa Helton Shively.
Book design and typesetting by Chelsea Hansen.
Cover design by Marie Turner.
Printing by BookMobile.